ECK WISDOM

on

Health
and Healing

ECK WISDOM

on

Health and Healing

HAROLD KLEMP

ECKANKAR

Minneapolis

www.Eckankar.org

ECK Wisdom on Health and Healing

Copyright © 2006 ECKANKAR

The terms ECKANKAR, ECK, EK, MAHANTA, SOUL TRAVEL, and VAIRAGI, among others, are trademarks of ECKANKAR, PO Box 2000, Chanhassen, MN 55317-2000 USA.   190537

Printed in USA

Photo of Sri Harold Klemp (page 78) by Art Galbraith
Cover photo by Jane Burgess
Fourth printing—2019

Library of Congress Cataloging-in-Publication Data
Names: Klemp, Harold, author.
Title: ECK wisdom on health and healing / Harold Klemp.
Other titles: Spiritual wisdom on health and healing
Description: Second. | Chanhassen, Minnesota : Eckankar, 2019. | Summary: "ECK Wisdom on Health and Healing "Author Harold Klemp, spiritual leader of Eckankar, helps you see yourself and your state of health from a higher perspective. Where does healing come from? How can you heal the past to help yourself now?" -- Provided by publisher.
Identifiers: LCCN 2019039446 | ISBN 9781570434877 (paperback)
Subjects: LCSH: Eckankar (Organization) | Spiritual healing.
Classification: LCC BP605.E3 K57445 2019 | DDC 299/.93--dc23
LC record available at https://lccn.loc.gov/2019039446

∞ This paper meets the requirements of ANSI/NISO Z39.48-1992 (Permanence of Paper).

CONTENTS

WHERE DOES HEALING COME FROM?

We are in some very interesting times in human history. The unfoldment of the human race has come a long way in the last hundred years. As a result of this creativity, there is a whole new world of energy, a whole new world of possibilities.

In these times, many people are looking to a variety of sources of healing. Traditional doctors are still very necessary, but people are also finding their way to alternative methods of healing.

Why are they doing this?

Because the level of consciousness is higher. In the past, people went to a certain doctor to heal their troubles. But troubles of the present and future are going to take different kinds of doctors to address and heal them.

Remember that the main healing comes not from any outer source. Any true, humble doctor knows that healing does not come through pills, herbs, or anything else. It comes through the divine power—through the power of God getting through in some way to one individual to help bring about a healing. The individual is only a channel for this healing power that knows better than anyone else what you need.

Divine Spirit often heals through the field of medicine and guides you to the doctor who is right for your condition. Yet the ways of healing by Divine Spirit are truly endless. And many times, an individual who has received relief does not connect it back to Spirit, but feels he has stumbled upon help by chance.

Many of you, however, are more ready and able to begin moving seriously on the path to God than you have ever been before.

This means that you learn to take responsibility for your own life, for your own health, for your own economics. You try to become self-sufficient. We have strength inside to accept the spiritual power that's here to help us come into accord with these strange new forces that are all around us.

All the help that comes to us is from the Holy Spirit, whether it comes in a dream or through the help of a friend or a doctor. The trick is the discrimination you need: to tell what's good for you and what's not good for you.

This comes by listening to your heart.

THE PURPOSE OF HEALING

*T*he purpose of healing transcends the cure of a bodily condition. There is a spiritual reason the illness occurred.

The process of spiritual healing teaches us something about ourselves we didn't know before. When the eyes are in trouble, we have to ask, What am I *not* seeing about my spiritual life that is causing me difficulty with my eyesight?

You see, the approach assumes responsibility for whatever is wrong. Once we're willing to shoulder the blame for our thoughts and actions, the inner forces can begin to heal us, even as our understanding of the causes becomes known to us through our dreams or other means.

It's pointless to debate the merits of medical doctors versus chiropractors or herbalists. Your karma differs from that of other people. You as an individual have to find the healing modality that is right for you.

Even that can change with time. Your state of consciousness today is not the same as it used to be or as it will be in two weeks or a couple of years from now.

As karma surfaces, it works out through the weakest point in our body. As quickly as we can release our attachment to whatever is hurting us, we allow the karma to pass off quickly, and our health stays balanced.

The key is to stay in tune with Divine Spirit. Through the Spiritual Exercises of ECK, you can be aware of the hints and nudges and whisperings of the Holy Spirit as It tries to guide you to the next step to take at any given point.

One of the things you learn is that there is always a way. Always.

The Spiritual Exercises of ECK build your faith in the Spirit of God and Its power to do miracles. There's a story of two blind men who came to Jesus, calling after him to heal them. Jesus asked, "Do you think I can do this thing?" They both said yes. Jesus touched their eyes and said, "According to your faith be it unto you." And their eyes were opened. Their great faith had opened them to the healing power of God.

Healing came, the Bible says, because their eyes were opened. But what actually happens is the heart opens. Some people get a healing, and some people don't. Some people can open their hearts, and others have no idea what that means.

I recognize that the Holy Spirit is the healer. It may come through a book, it may come through a doctor. These things all work together. It's up to us to accept the gift and the love that's so freely given.

We must have the awareness to do so. Often it takes pain and dire necessity before we even come to the point where we say, My eyes are open. I'm looking, I'm looking. Then when the blessings—the different methods of healing—show up, we recognize them as the next step.

To get an inkling of how to open your heart so you can have the guidance of the Holy Spirit help you in your daily life, read on.

EFFECT OF AN ATTITUDE

A woman I'll call Lydia had a sudden onset of severe headaches and stomach pains. Only after the pain became almost too great to bear did she realize the tie-in with a karmic condition caused by a certain attitude she had developed years ago.

She called her father, a doctor who lived in another town, and described her symptoms.

"It sounds like you're suffering from migraines," he said.

The headaches had come on so quickly that Lydia hadn't even considered that possibility.

One evening while doing a spiritual exercise, the reason for these severe headaches came to her. Her pain had opened up a childhood memory of her mother, who had suffered with migraines. Her mother's pain was so severe she became addicted to drugs, and for all these years Lydia had resented her mother for this weakness.

Suddenly the very condition that had caused her to feel such resentment toward her mother finally came to the surface.

The Spiritual Exercises of ECK gave Lydia the strength as Soul to understand and, more importantly, to accept the reason for her pain. She could now look at herself honestly and admit that she had formed a negative attitude simply because she didn't understand the severity of her mother's pain; she had lacked the experience by which to gauge it.

From that point on, Lydia's condition began to improve, and at last report the migraines were gone. A spiritual healing had taken hold.

Love and Gratitude, Keys to Good Health

$\mathcal{K}$risty would go out running every day for health reasons. One day she decided to run in a marathon, and a friend volunteered to help.

Every five miles her friend would meet her to give her water to drink. This good-hearted friend ran the last six and a half miles with Kristy. The friend had a water pack strapped on her back and also another pack with nutritional fluids, so Kristy could have nutrition and strength as she finished the marathon.

I found it hard to imagine anyone running with that much weight on her back for six and a half miles. I thought that was quite a feat in itself. But, it was given as a gift of love, and Kristy accepted it in the very same way.

Another day, after her daily run for exercise, Kristy came inside all worn out. But then her cat Misha gave her a gift of love.

Kristy had her own nutrition business, which was very challenging. All her cares about it weighed upon her. And this particular day she was worried. Should she keep her business, or should she accept the job a nutrition company had offered her, which would pay very well? The downside was it would mean a lot of travel.

She was sitting there wondering about what to do, tired out from her run, and even more tired from the worries of her business and the decision about what to do with her future. Then Misha, her Siamese cat, nudged her.

He had his favorite toy in his mouth,

and he was saying, "Hey, it's time to play. Lighten up. This is my gift of love to you."

This made all the difference in the world to Kristy. Her cares lifted as she recognized and accepted this gift of love. It was a healing gift from one of God's creatures. Another Soul. Yes, animals are Soul too.

You'll notice I'm very careful not to say animals *have* a soul. Animals *are* Soul, just as you are Soul. You cannot possess Soul. Soul is free.

A Simple Exercise
to Help Heal Yourself

$\mathcal{P}$eople are usually too busy count-
ing the things they don't have. They notice
how much more money their neighbor has,
how much further ahead in spiritual unfoldment someone else is, and so on.

But if we stop to count our blessings, to
realize how much we do have and be grateful for it, then the heart is kept open to love
and all the gifts that love brings, including
the possibility of healing.

There is a technique for this, but unlike
other spiritual exercises, it does not have a
beginning, middle, and end. This technique
involves attitude, and it is one that must

13

be lived. In a word, it's called gratitude.

The power of gratitude opens the heart to allow love to enter. But once the love comes in and we receive the gifts of Spirit and of life, the way to keep the gifts flowing is through an ongoing spirit of gratitude.

I wish there were some easy technique I could give you to feel gratitude. There are times when it will seem difficult, but it's really as simple as appreciating what you have in your life. If there is someone you love, let that person know how you feel. Say thank you to your mate or your child even when you don't feel well.

If you can just stop and be grateful for the blessings that are before you, your heart will open to love. Then the blessings can keep coming!

HEALING THE PAST
CAN HELP YOU NOW

Sometimes the healing that takes place has almost a comical aspect to it, except for the fact that there's pain underneath.

A woman had left her husband. I'll call her Judith to safeguard her privacy. The marriage wasn't working out to her satisfaction. She had a feeling of sadness about the whole thing. One night in contemplation, she asked the Mahanta (my inner side, her spiritual guide) if she could have a healing from this sadness.

Judith worked part-time in offices, here, there, and wherever. But as a sideline, she was an extra in TV shows. The next day her agent called and said he had an opening for her. The studio people sent transportation for her, so she was soon in a car going to the location where she was to be an extra in this TV series.

When they got to the location, Judith went inside to the set. And who did she meet? The first person she ran into was her husband.

Her husband was in the acting business too. He worked with an entirely different agency, but he was an extra for this same TV series on this very same day. So there they were, together. Just the night before, Judith had asked the Mahanta for a healing from this problem in their relationship.

Pretty soon the assistant director came up and put them at their proper places on the set. The assistant director was working up imaginary scenarios.

He said to the husband, "Now, you're

going to be her ex-husband. Sit right here beside her."

The husband and wife were looking at each other, thinking, *What's going on? This is so crazy! This man couldn't have set this up better if he knew the truth.* The assistant director was just creating these scenarios in his mind, or so he thought. But Divine Spirit was at work.

So for the whole day, this couple was together on the set.

Interestingly enough, the scene took place at an Alcoholics Anonymous meeting. After the day of filming was over, Judith was talking to a friend about it. "You know," the friend pointed out, "AA is about people who are trying to heal something in the past."

On the set, the couple was indeed healing something from the past. The assistant director thought he was creating these great fictional scenes, but he didn't know the real husband and wife were in front of him. You have to view these setups with a wry sense of humor.

Divine Spirit has a way of doing exactly what is right for everyone concerned at the moment. It's not always funny at the time, and it catches people off guard. But sometimes when we're caught off guard, our hearts open. Then the healing can begin.

It doesn't happen overnight; it may take months. But at least the seed of healing is planted.

DREAMS CAN BRING HEALING

A woman I'll call Lyn was traveling to the ECK European Seminar in Germany. On the flight, her two seat companions were younger women, in their midtwenties, dressed in black leather jackets. They had rings through their noses. They were laughing and chatting and sipping their wine.

Lyn was sitting there thinking, *There's a generation gap here. I don't think I have a whole lot in common with these two young women.* So Lyn mostly read or slept while the plane was en route.

Soon the flight attendants began serving a meal. The young woman next to Lyn got a salad. By accident, the young woman bumped her salad, and pieces of lettuce, tomato, and cucumber went flying. A slice of tomato even landed on Lyn's shoe. She looked down and began to laugh. The young woman started laughing too, as they were picking pieces of shredded produce off their clothes. Then they began to talk.

These two young women were not just friends; they happened to be twins. As they were talking to Lyn, one of the young women said that some extraordinary things had happened in her life that were beyond explanation. Somehow, the conversation turned to Eckankar and dreams.

The young woman had a boyfriend who, in a previous relationship, had had his heart broken. The pain was so great that one night when he was ready to go to sleep, he asked God, "Please help me; take this pain away." During the night, a light suddenly appeared at the foot of his bed. This light was so bright it lit up the whole room.

The young man wasn't afraid of it, but he wondered, *What is this light?*

As she heard this story, Lyn knew immediately: This was the Light of God.

When the young man woke up in the morning, he was surprised to find his pain was entirely gone. This light had come and healed him. And he wondered about it. He had no answers.

This was one of the extraordinary things the two young women had come across. It was no accident the ECK (Divine Spirit) had placed Lyn in the seat beside them. Nor was it an accident that one of the young women tipped her salad over or that the conversation turned to Eckankar.

Sometimes the ECK works this way, when people allow themselves to tune in to the Holy Spirit. ECK is the Holy Spirit, Divine Spirit.

How do you tune in to It in Eckankar?

With the Spiritual Exercises of ECK.

That's our form of prayer. It's a form of contemplation where we don't try to tell God what to do. We listen to hear what God's Voice is saying to us.

A Spiritual Exercise to Heal Yourself Using Dreams

*H*ere is a way to heal yourself that begins with a spiritual exercise. At bedtime, sing the word *HU* (pronounced like the word *hue*). Softly sing this ancient name for God for five to ten minutes. Also create a mental picture of your problem. See it as a simple cartoon. Beside it, place another image of the condition as you feel it should be. Then let yourself fall asleep as usual.

Keep a record of your dreams. Make a short note about every dream you recall upon awakening. Also be alert during the day for clues about your problem from other people. The Holy Spirit works through them too.

Try this for a week. The second week, if you've had no luck finding a solution to your problem, extend the bedtime spiritual exercise to fifteen or twenty minutes. Take a rest the third week. Repeat this cycle until you succeed.

A solution exists for every challenge to our peace of mind. There is always a way, somehow. What holds us back from happiness is our lack of faith in the mighty power of the Holy Spirit to address our most humble needs.

HEALING POWER OF THE BLUE LIGHT

*A*llen, let's call him, worked in a very high position with the largest commercial bank in Canada. He was thirty-nine at the time. Ever since he was fourteen, he had been searching for truth.

Four years earlier, Allen had been driving at night from his aunt's home, going to his mother's, a distance of about three miles. He was very concerned about his aunt's health. As he drove these three miles, he asked God for spiritual guidance. He wanted to get some help because his aunt's failing health really upset him. This aunt had been like a second mother to him.

In the last mile before Allen got to his mother's home, something happened that shook him to his roots. Suddenly, everything—all the lights in the night—turned blue.

Car headlights were blue, storefronts were blue, streetlights were blue, the lights on his dash were all blue. He pulled over. "Must be some kind of a neurological problem going on here," he said. He sat on the side of the road and looked around. Other cars were going by, and nobody seemed to notice these blue lights all around. It really startled him.

Allen began looking for an answer, and he searched for the next four years. What had happened that night? What were those blue lights? He sensed there was something spiritual about the experience.

He looked throughout Christianity and then Tibetan Buddhism. He went to the highest lamas in that faith, and he asked,

"What is the blue light?"

No one could tell him, but he kept looking and looking.

One day someone gave him *ECKANKAR— Ancient Wisdom for Today*, and in the book he found an explanation for the blue light. He realized that the Mahanta, the Living ECK Master had answered his call for spiritual assistance.

You may be wondering how a blue light would help him.

This is the wake-up call the Ancient One gives to Souls when they're ready to begin the journey back home to God. In one way or another, the Mahanta, the Inner Master, will approach the individual. The Mahanta has approached each of you; otherwise you wouldn't be reading this.

It doesn't mean that you're going to be an ECKist the rest of your life. Some people may say, "I have no more use for Eckankar." Or, "This is the strangest, most preposterous

27

stuff I've ever heard. I'm going back to my old church." They go back there for a while. But at some point, either in this lifetime or another lifetime, they're going to be in such a circumstance where they're going to need to search for truth again.

They'll be in a time of need.

This is when the Inner Master will approach and in some way try to awaken the individual. Again, that person has the right to either accept or reject the wake-up call and the spiritual healing it can bring.

A Spiritual Exercise Using Light for Healing

*I*n your spiritual exercises there are two things you can use for healing. One is the orange light, and the other is the blue light. You may wish to experiment with them. Some people are successful in this kind of healing, and others are better off seeing a doctor. It depends on you.

The orange light is mostly for the physical body. Go into contemplation in your usual way, whether you sit up or lie down. Using the imaginative power, which is the God Force or the seeing power of Soul, shut your eyes and visualize the Audible Life Stream. This is the pure white Light of God, a composite of all the colors.

Now visualize a ray coming off of It. It's very much like using a prism to see the spectrum of colors.

The ray you see is orange, which applies to physical health. With your eyes closed, visualize this orange stream coming through you. Just let it flow to the area in your body that is diseased, afflicted, or injured. You can do this for twenty minutes.

This is a healing technique. But you do it only for yourself; don't go out and blast orange light at other people.

The blue light is another way of healing, but it is for the inner bodies—the Astral, Causal, Mental, and Etheric. These are the bodies of the psychic worlds below the Soul Plane.

Here again, you use a technique similar to that of the orange light. And I'll repeat this: Do it only for yourself, never for another person.

Close your eyes and visualize the blue

light coming into the heart center. This light is known as the Blue Light of the Mahanta. The Mahanta Consciousness is the highest state of consciousness known to man. The blue light is for the calming and healing of the inner man—your emotions and your mind. Along with this technique, get plenty of physical rest.

The blue light is not something that is created out of the ethers from some source alien to yourself. It comes from your own God Worlds, and you are now becoming aware of it.

Let this healing Light of God come in and work on the area you feel needs help. Or just let It flow into the Spiritual Eye (area above and between the eyebrows). As It washes and cleanses the impurities, It will start to uplift you from the materialism and karma that you have created for yourself through ignorance of God's laws.

A true spiritual healing first heals the

spiritual condition that caused the symptoms to appear in the physical body. You have to understand that when you use the orange light, it may not bring a miraculous healing, such as the reshaping of limbs, or anything like this. But it may lead you to a better doctor.

Dream Visitor Brings Help

A Nigerian woman I'll call Sarah first heard of Eckankar on a recording of a televised talk I'd given some years earlier.

Sarah had caught the last segment of a three-part program introducing the ECK teachings. To her utter amazement, a perfect six-pointed blue star replaced my face on the TV screen. She recognized it as a spiritual gift, and it was a great inspiration to her. And so she drove to an ECK Center to borrow some books. It was there that she noticed an event taking place in the next room. The center's host invited her to stay and attend the event, which happened to be an ECK Light and Sound Service.

In the room used for the service, Sarah

noticed pictures of the ECK Masters. Right off, one of the pictures drew her attention. This is her story:

Some six years earlier, Sarah had suffered grave injuries in a car accident, which left her unconscious for four days. She showed no response whatever to medical treatments, so the doctors decided to disconnect her life-support system.

At that very critical moment, an old man came to her on the inner planes. He told her to ask the doctors for a bed next to the wall.

Sarah stirred from the unconscious state and made the request. No sooner had the staff moved her to the new location than she slipped into a quite normal sleep. But this applied only to her physical body. In a subtle, inner body she awoke under a wondrous and most beautiful covering of silvery stars. Dancing, sparkling lights covered her bed and the walls.

Ever since that experience, Sarah felt a

deep longing of some kind in her heart. But a longing for what, she couldn't say.

In the days and weeks to come, Sarah showed a remarkable recovery. Her doctor warned she'd carry severe deformities from her injuries, yet in six months all her bones had healed, much to her doctor's surprise.

So it was on that day in the ECK Center Sarah chanced upon the picture of a certain ECK Master. To her surprise and delight, she learned the identity of the old man who'd come to her in the hospital a full six years earlier. It was none other than the venerable ECK Master Fubbi Quantz.

Fubbi Quantz is one of the wonderful ECK Masters who assist the Mahanta, the Living ECK Master. People have looked to these spiritual guides since the beginning of time for guidance, protection, and divine love.

Fubbi's picture was the final, long-awaited sign that Sarah's spiritual seeking had reached an end. The ECK teachings were like a cool, healing salve to her once-restless, seeking heart.

SPIRITUAL HEALING MAY COME UNEXPECTEDLY

$\mathcal{E}$dna (not her real name) had a grandchild who died, and this left her distraught. So this woman's son asked one of the ECKists, "Do you have grief groups in Eckankar?"

The ECKist said, "No, but we do have ESAs. These are ECK Spiritual Aides." They simply listen to the problem of an individual, pretty much the same as the confessor in the Catholic Church, except people are not expected to confess here. Whenever they have any trouble, they can request an ESA session to simply air it. The ESA does nothing—just listens. If the Holy Spirit wants to change something in that person's life, It does so in Its own way at Its own time.

After she had an ESA session, Edna felt much better. Years later she said, "It saved my life."

It was the answer for her at that particular time. She and her son began to go to some of the ECK Light and Sound Services. In fact, they went quite regularly. Then she joined a four-week class, "Getting Answers from God through Past Lives, Dreams, and Soul Travel."

The death of Edna's grandchild had happened several years before, but she was still carrying the pain. In all the time she went to the ECK services, she hadn't become a member of Eckankar. She was still waiting for the spiritual leader, myself, to drop the other shoe.

She wondered, *Is this guy going to try to coerce people? Is he going to try to deceive them? Make them members?*

No, because then I carry your load for you. I like spiritual freedom, so I won't carry the load of an unwilling person. Whenever you trick a person into following your path, you take on part of that individual's burden. I don't want to do that. I'm into spiritual freedom.

At the class "Getting Answers from God through Past Lives, Dreams, and Soul Travel," the facilitators showed a video of a talk I'd given some time ago, "The Right of Choice." In it I told the story of an African father whose child had died in a hospital. Hearing this story finally released the woman from her grief.

It gave her an understanding of the reason for the death of her grandchild. The healing came through a back door, years after the tragic event in her own life.

The Holy Spirit knows when you're ready to handle the information of why something happens. It may be a few days, it may be a moment, it may be a couple years, or many years. It may come very directly and, very often, in a way that is totally unexpected.

Questions and Answers

*A*s spiritual leader of Eckankar, I get thousands of letters from seekers of truth around the world. All want direct and useful answers about how to travel the road to God. I reply personally to many of these letters.

Here are several questions I've been asked about health and healing.

Read on for clues that may help you.

Can Sound Heal?

I am having some health problems after enjoying a strong body for most of my life. The Sound of God, the divine Sound Current, is very loud. Am I going through a spiritual or physical change?

You mention a change of health and an increase of the Sound Current, that aspect of the Holy Spirit one can hear. The natural effect of a changing consciousness can show up as both physical and emotional. It requires us to adjust our habits of eating and perhaps even the spiritual exercises.

In my case, I found that aging had an effect upon my feelings of well-being. It forced me to develop new dietary habits. I eventually gave up caffeine stimulants, such as are found in coffee, many soft drinks, and even chocolate. The stimulants, on top of my increasing spiritual awareness, made me too sensitive to the Sound of God.

We want the Sound in our lives, but too much of It can render us physically unable to carry on with our daily life. That means we must find a new balance. This means changing our habits.

Go about this rationally. Look at the foods you eat, for instance, then eliminate one food or drink that seems least useful to you spiritually. Continue to eat and drink your other foods and beverages. Watch for a few days if the removal of a certain food had any beneficial effect upon your feelings of well-being. If it did, don't use that food for several weeks. Later, you may wish to experiment: try to eat it again, but observe the effect it has upon your feelings of well-being.

Follow this plan with a second item of food or drink that seems *least* beneficial for your physical or spiritual good. Go slow. You don't want to make massive changes to your diet. It could be too much of a shock to your body, and that would create unnecessary health conditions.

In effect, you're treating your body as a science lab. What you see there is unique: a reflection of your expanding state of consciousness. While making observations on your food and beverage habits, be sure to get any help you see necessary from experts in nutrition and health care.

We are a state of consciousness. Everyone and everything in our personal and universal world has an effect upon us. We want to become aware of what these effects are. Then we can sort through them, nurturing the good ones and discarding the bad.

What Is the Difference between Psychic and Spiritual Healing?

I'd like a greater understanding of the difference between psychic healers and other kinds of healers.

Regular healers help fix problems people cause themselves by putting a Band-Aid on them. If you go to a doctor for a cut, he cleans it and applies a bandage until it can heal naturally. He does not try to tamper with a spiritual condition he is not qualified to heal, which psychic healers often try to do and thereby set up more causes to be worked out as more problems.

A difference between psychic healing and spiritual healing is that psychic healing leaves you in the same state of consciousness, perhaps temporarily alleviating symptoms caused by an attitude you hold. However, spiritual healing helps change the attitude which caused the problem, so it can go away and not recur.

The problem surrounding healing is karmic. The ill person once broke a divine principle through ignorance. Psychic healers can ease the symptoms for a while, but eventually the sickness surfaces again with a new face.

In the meantime, the healer is accruing the karma from all the people he heals with the psychic force. Someday the debt comes due. There is more to healing than erasing the outer symptoms for a few months or years, or until the passion of the mind that lies behind the illness produces the next symptom of arthritis, cancer, or some other disease.

When the Living ECK Master is asked to help, he puts the entire matter into the hands of the ECK (Holy Spirit).

Spirit, in Its divine wisdom, sees whether or not the individual has learned to control the mental aberration that made him ill. If not, there is no healing. After all, Divine Spirit wants only the education of Soul so It can be a Co-worker with God.

Does Spiritual Fasting Help You Heal?

Can you give me some idea how enlightenment comes into Soul and heals the inner bodies, and what techniques help with this?

Enlightenment is a gentle thing if it's right, if you're ready for it. It gives you a different viewpoint, a different state of consciousness.

This also occurs when we do a spiritual

fast and keep our thoughts on God, the Mahanta, or something spiritual. You'll notice that when you are on a spiritual fast, you treat people differently at work and at home. You're in a different state of awareness that day. You're pulled out of the routine or rut the mind likes.

This actually works off karma. The hold of the material world, the attachments, are not as strong on you. This gives you a little more freedom of choice. It puts you in charge of your own life in subtle ways. Other people can feel this.

Suppose there is something going on at work, something that's not too smooth for you. You can do a spiritual fast for a couple of days. You'll find that your attitude and your very words are different. You're not creating karma the way you were before.

Most of our problems are self-made. When things go wrong, if we take responsibility and do something that gives us greater understanding, life becomes easier.

This is how it should be, rather than having someone always giving us spiritual, emotional, or physical healings.

Is There a Cure for Insomnia?

Over the years, I've had a problem with insomnia that has gotten more severe. I have called on many specialists, but the insomnia is so all-prevailing that it is literally ruining my life. Can you point me in any direction?

I don't often like to bring up past lives, for people usually have enough resources at hand in their life to get a start on their health problem. With science so much in the forefront today, people tend to overlook influences from past lives because the idea seems hokey.

Nevertheless, perhaps a look into your past will give you an understanding of your inability to rest.

Some geologists poke fun at the notion

of Atlantis, since none of their drilling into the ocean floor shows it to ever have been above water. Anyway, the civilization was very advanced in many ways that would make science today envious. But, as a whole, people at that time were spiritually in what we'd call a state of infantile emotional development.

In short, they were efficient to a T, but the consciousness then had only the beginnings of what we'd call compassion and humanity. Thus it became a common practice during the decline of Atlantis for doctors to perform euthanasia upon patients who were old, sickly, or malformed according to the standards of beauty in vogue then.

Somehow, you escaped notice of the authorities, even though you had a misshapen back, which left you in a constantly bent-over position. No one was too concerned about your appearance because you were a rural laborer, the equivalent of a migrant farmworker. Such labor was necessary because the maturing Atlantean society was much like ours today in that everybody was becoming too refined to dirty their hands at manual labor.

But you grew old and fell sick in the fields. This brought you to the attention of the medical people.

It was determined that your useful life as a laborer was at an end. As with so many other unfortunates, a day and hour was set when you would be administered a drug that would put you into an eternal sleep. The medical people treated you like an object without feelings, speaking clinically—without grace—about the removal of your body and belongings the morning after.

You were terrified of what amounted to a death sentence, and this fear is the reason for your fear of sleep. While you've suffered from insomnia for a long time, it's gotten worse as you approach a condition of aging similar to the one in Atlantis. The aging is the trigger.

Soul cannot die. You did not know that in Atlantis.

To bend this condition of fear back to a more reasonable place, I suggest you find a way to be an aide or a volunteer who works with small *children*. Best of all would be to work with emotionally—not physically—handicapped children, so you can come to terms with the emotionally bankrupt Atlanteans who caused you so much trouble in the past.

You need to feel and see the continuity of life. Mainly, you must find a way to give your love to little ones. You now see yourself as the center of your world; you must make others the object of your love, which has to pour out from you. It must become unlocked and flow out into the world.

It may be hard to do this at first, so start small.

How Can I Restructure and Heal My Life?

My husband left me suddenly almost five years ago, and I cannot get my life nor my finances straightened out. After reading many books I was beginning to develop psychic abilities, but then they stopped. Please check my Akashic records to see why these things are happening.

While the Akashic, or past-life, records of anyone are important in determining certain causes and effects in his life, most of the problems that arise from the past cannot be solved simply by a knowledge of it. Otherwise most psychic readers who are good at reading the Akashic records would be able to help people straighten out unhappy lives at will.

But this does not happen. Somebody must have the knowledge of how to begin unwinding the intricate karma that has brought one to the present-day trouble.

This is a spiritual skill that is known to very few of those who can read the past records.

The Adepts in ECK have a single purpose in mind when a seeker comes to them for relief: to give that Soul the opportunity for achieving wisdom, power, and freedom, three attributes of God-Realization. This means simply that an individual learns to be like the Adepts, enjoying a 360-degree viewpoint, the center of which is a love for all living things.

When one gains a degree of this love, he is himself able to restructure his life along lines that suit him. He is no longer at the mercy of destiny and the blind fates, but becomes a knowing being who understands the secret laws that govern his affairs. He is like the sailor who knows the ocean currents; he can chart a course to a destination and be quite certain of getting there in his sailboat.

Most of the cause for your present

trouble is indeed from the past, but not in the desertion of your mate then or now. There is a tendency for you to lean upon others, to let them think for you.

When this rubber crutch is leaned upon, it gives way and you fall down, at the mercy of every sort of misfortune that can be imagined. Therefore, the lesson that Soul must learn in this case is to find a more substantial inner support than It has in the past.

Your problems with failing finances are simply due to a lack of knowledge about the ins and outs of finance. I suggest you make an effort to learn about the financial areas that would be most helpful to you in the immediate future. If you let go and give your concerns to Divine Spirit, you will be guided to the best avenue to take next. Look over all the different ways open to you to learn about finance: local courses in the community, help from a friend who is well off in money matters, or books in the library.

There is no more magic about setting oneself up financially than there is for an experienced cook to bake a cake. There is a recipe for success no matter what field one is in. Failure, like a fallen angel-food cake, means the cook overlooked something important in the baking process that a better cook does by second nature.

Too many people want to use the psychic field as a shortcut to improving their lives. They feel there is a magical route that will leapfrog them over the hardship of self-discipline. The psychic field is set in an unstable force and will fail just as a person thinks he has a certain method for predicting the future down pat.

But, then, what is life all about? It's learning firsthand about the things that are harmful to us.

Yet this knowledge alone is not enough

to keep us out of trouble or to keep us from getting ill. We also have to exercise the self-discipline to keep away from the harmful things.

Of course, our rate of success or failure at self-discipline varies. Sometimes we are good at it; other times, not so good. Life allows us the opportunity to learn at our own pace.

In ECK, I want to show people how to become open channels for Divine Spirit. Remember, Soul has come into the lower worlds in many different incarnations in order to learn to be a Co-worker with God. A mechanical method of restructuring your life will fail unless there is also an upliftment in consciousness.

THE GREATEST CREATIVE FORCE YOU CAN USE FOR HEALING

*Y*ou will learn that the path to God is not one of a group. You are on this path to God yourself.

You may be a member of a group that is very large or very small, or you may go all by yourself. But you are on this journey to God. The only important thing on this journey is you and God. Once you've established the correct relationship between yourself and God, then you're able to go back out into the world and serve all God's creatures. And you will serve with love, kindness, compassion, and understanding.

Because you've walked in those mocca-
sins before, you can help others by listening. You've been there. And there are others
who can help you because they've been
where you are now.

The greatest creative force you can use
on your behalf is either contemplation or
prayer. I suggest singing *HU* (pronounced
like the word *hue* and sung in a long, drawn-
out breath).

HU is a love song to God. It uplifts and
purifies us of the evils that make life too
much to bear. It heals our wounds, soothes
our brow: sweet, but mighty, name of God.

In all heaven and earth, no name is
mightier than HU. It can lift the grieving
heart to a temple of solace. A companion
in trouble, it is likewise a friend in times of
prosperity. And is it any wonder, for HU is
Soul's most precious gift from God.

Anytime you sing *HU* as a love offering
to the Lord of all creation, your heart fills

with the Light and Sound of God. They are the twin aspects of ECK, the Holy Spirit. HU, the name of God, brings us into a holy alliance with the Light and Sound, the Word of God. Should the worlds tremble and all else fail, HU carries us into the ocean of God's love and mercy.

In time, people everywhere will have the chance to sing this age-old, universal name for God. This is a new cycle in the spiritual history of the human community.

So sing *HU* softly, gently. It is for those who desire true love, true freedom, wisdom, and truth.

Next Steps in Spiritual Exploration

- **Try a spiritual exercise.**
  Review the spiritual exercises in this book or on our website. Experiment with them.

- **Browse our website: www.Eckankar.org.**
  Watch videos; get free books, answers to FAQs, and more info.

- **Attend a spiritual event in your area.**
  Visit "Eckankar around the World" on our website.

- **Begin your journey** with the Eckankar spiritual self-discovery courses that come with membership.

- **Read additional books** about the ECK teachings.

- **Call us:** Call 1-800-LOVE GOD (1-800-568-3463, toll-free, automated) or (952) 380-2200 (direct).

- **Write to:** ECKANKAR, Dept. BK61, PO Box 2000, Chanhassen, MN 55317-2000 USA.

FOR FURTHER READING
By Harold Klemp

The Spiritual Exercises of ECK

This book is a staircase with 131 steps leading to the doorway to spiritual freedom, self-mastery, wisdom, and love. A comprehensive volume of spiritual exercises for every need.

ECK Wisdom on Conquering Fear

Would having more courage and confidence help you make the most of this lifetime?

Going far beyond typical self-help advice, this book invites you to explore divine love as the antidote to anxiety and the doorway to inner freedom.

You will discover ways

to identify the karmic roots of fear and align with your highest ideals.

Use this book to soar beyond your limitations and reap the benefits of self-mastery.

Live life to its fullest potential!

ECK Wisdom on Dreams

This dream study will help you be more *awake* than you've ever been!

ECK Wisdom on Dreams reveals the most ancient of dream teachings for a richer and more productive life today.

In this dynamic book, author Harold Klemp shows you how to remember your dreams, apply dream wisdom to everyday situations, recognize prophetic dreams, and more.

You will be introduced to the art of dream interpretation and offered techniques to discover the treasures of your inner worlds.

ECK Wisdom on Inner Guidance

Looking for answers, guidance, protection?

Help can come as a nudge, a dream, a vision, or a quiet voice within you. This book offers new ways to connect with the ever-present guidance of ECK, the Holy Spirit. Start today!

Discover how to listen to the Voice of God; attune to your true self; work with an inner guide; benefit from dreams, waking dreams, and Golden-tongued Wisdom; and ignite your creativity to solve problems.

Each story, technique, and spiritual exercise is a doorway to greater confidence and love for life.

Open your heart, and let God's voice speak to you!

ECK Wisdom on Karma and Reincarnation

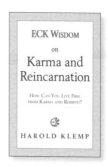

Have you lived before? What is the real meaning of life?

Discover your divine destiny—to move beyond the limits of karma and reincarnation and gain spiritual freedom.

This book reveals the purpose of living and the keys to spiritual growth.

You'll find answers to age-old questions about fate, destiny, and free will. These gems of wisdom can enhance your relationships, health, and happiness—and offer the chance to resolve all your karma in this lifetime!

ECK Wisdom on Life after Death

All that lies ahead is already within your heart.

ECK Wisdom on Life after Death invites you to explore the eternal nature of *you*!

Author Harold Klemp offers you new perspectives

on seeing heaven before you die, meeting with departed loved ones, near-death experiences, getting help from spiritual guides, animals in heaven, and dealing with grief.

Try the techniques and spiritual exercise included in this book to find answers and explore the secrets of life after death—for yourself.

ECK Wisdom on Solving Problems

Problems? Problems! Why do we have so many? What causes them? Can we avoid them?

Author Harold Klemp, the spiritual leader of Eckankar, can help you answer these questions and more. His sense of humor and practical approach offer spiritual keys to unlock the secrets to effective problem solving. Learn creative, time-tested techniques to

- Find the root cause of a problem
- Change your viewpoint and overcome difficulties
- Conquer your fears

- Work beyond symptoms to solutions
- Kindle your creativity
- Master your karma, past and present
- Receive spiritual guidance that can transform the way you see yourself and your life

ECK Wisdom on Spiritual Freedom

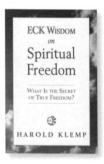

Are you everything you want to be? You came into this life to spread your wings and live in freedom—heart, mind, and Soul!

Author Harold Klemp puts the tools of spiritual freedom firmly in your grasp:

- Keys to embrace the highest expression of who you really are
- Techniques to tap into the divine Life Force for unlimited creativity and problem solving
- New paradigms to reveal the power of loving yourself, God, and all of life

What would you give for the secret of true freedom? Consider this book a ticket to an unexpected destination—the heart of your being.

Open your wings and prepare for flight!

ECK Wisdom on Soul Travel

Where do you go when you close your eyes?

Nowhere? Are you sure?

What about when you daydream?

You go places, don't you?

What about when you close your eyes at night—and dream? When dreams seem more real than everyday life?

That's Soul Travel. It's a natural process that opens the door to the incredible universes where we truly live and have our being. You are Soul, a divine spark of God. The more attention you give to this wonderful truth, the closer you get to the very heart of God.

You learn how to grow in love and awareness. And that's what life is all about, isn't it?

ECK Wisdom on Soul Travel gives you tools to experiment with and introduces you to a spiritual guide to help show you the road to your infinite future—a road that courses through every moment of your daily life.

Take a peek, and explore your own adventure of a lifetime!

Spiritual Wisdom on Prayer, Meditation, and Contemplation

Bring balance and wonder to your life!

This booklet is a portal to your direct, personal connection with Divine Spirit.

Harold Klemp shows how you can experience the powerful benefits of contemplation—"a conversation with the most secret, most genuine, and most mysterious part of yourself."

Move beyond traditional meditation via dynamic spiritual exercises. Learn about the uplifting chant of HU (an ancient holy name for God), visualization, creative imagination, and other active techniques.

Spiritual Wisdom on Relationships

Find the answers to common questions of the heart, including the truth about soul mates, how to strengthen a marriage, and how to know if a partnership is worth developing.

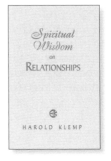

The spiritual exercises included in this booklet can help you break a pattern of poor relationships and find balance. You'll learn new ways to open your heart to love and enrich your relationship with God.

This booklet is a key for anyone wanting more love to give, more love to get, and better relationships with everyone in your life.

The Call of Soul

Discover how to find spiritual freedom in this lifetime and the infinite world of God's love for you. Includes a CD with dream and Soul Travel techniques.

Past Lives, Dreams, and Soul Travel

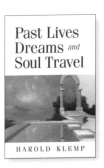

These stories and exercises help you find your true purpose, discover greater love than you've ever known, and learn that spiritual freedom is within reach.

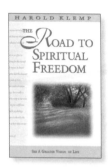

The Road to Spiritual Freedom, Mahanta Transcripts, Book 17

Sri Harold's wisdom and heart-opening stories of everyday people having extraordinary experiences tell of a secret truth at work in *your* life—there is divine purpose and meaning to every experience you have.

How to Survive Spiritually in Our Times, Mahanta Transcripts, Book 16

Discover how to reinvent yourself spiritually—to thrive in a changing world. Stories, tools, techniques, and spiritual insights to apply in your life now.

Autobiography of a Modern Prophet

This riveting story of Harold Klemp's climb up the Mountain of God will help you discover the keys to your own spiritual greatness.

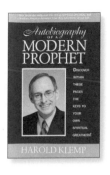

HU, the Most Beautiful Prayer

Singing *HU*, the ancient name for God, can open your heart and lead you to a new understanding of yourself. Includes a CD of the HU song.

Those Wonderful ECK Masters

Would you like to have *personal* experience with spiritual masters that people all over the world—since the beginning of time—have looked to for guidance, protection, and divine love? This book includes real-life stories and spiritual exercises to meet eleven ECK Masters.

The Spiritual Laws of Life

Learn how to keep in tune with your true spiritual nature. Spiritual laws reveal the behind-the-scenes forces at work in your daily life.

Available at bookstores, from online booksellers, or directly from Eckankar: www.ECKBooks.org; (952) 380-2222; ECKANKAR, Dept. BK61, PO Box 2000, Chanhassen, MN 55317-2000 USA.

GLOSSARY

Words set in SMALL CAPS are defined elsewhere in this glossary.

Blue Light How the MAHANTA often appears in the inner worlds to the CHELA or seeker.

chela A spiritual student, often a member of ECKANKAR.

ECK The Life Force, Holy Spirit, or Audible Life Current which sustains all life.

Eckankar *EHK-ahn-kahr* The Path of Spiritual Freedom. Also known as the Ancient Science of SOUL TRAVEL. A truly spiritual way of life for the individual in modern times. The teachings provide a framework for anyone to explore their own spiritual experiences. Established by PAUL TWITCHELL, the modern-day founder, in 1965. The word means Co-worker with God.

ECK Masters Spiritual Masters who can assist and protect people in their spiritual studies and travels. The ECK Masters are from a long line of God-Realized SOULS who know the responsibility that goes with spiritual freedom.

Fubbi Quantz The guardian of the SHARIYAT-KI-SUGMAD at the Katsupari Monastery in northern Tibet. He was the MAHANTA, the LIVING ECK MASTER during the time of Buddha, about 500 BC.

God-Realization The state of God Consciousness. Complete and conscious awareness of God.

HU *HYOO* The most ancient, secret name for God. It can be sung as a love song to God aloud or silently to oneself to align with God's love.

initiation Earned by a member of ECKANKAR through spiritual unfoldment and service to God. The initiation is a private ceremony in which the individual is linked to the Sound and Light of God.

Karma, Law of The Law of Cause and Effect, action and reaction, justice, retribution, and reward, which applies to the lower or psychic worlds: the Physical, Astral, Causal, Mental, and Etheric PLANES.

Klemp, Harold The present MAHANTA, the LIVING ECK MASTER. SRI Harold Klemp became the Mahanta, the Living ECK Master in 1981. His spiritual name is WAH Z.

Living ECK Master The spiritual leader of ECKANKAR. He leads SOUL back to God. He teaches in the physical world as the Outer Master, in the dream state as the Dream Master, and in the spiritual worlds as the Inner Master. Sri Harold Klemp became the Mahanta, the Living ECK Master in 1981.

Mahanta   An expression of the Spirit of God that is always with you. Sometimes seen as a Blue Light or Blue Star or in the form of the Mahanta, the Living ECK Master. The highest state of God Consciousness on earth, only embodied in the Living ECK Master. He is the Living Word.

planes   Levels of existence, such as the Physical, Astral, Causal, Mental, Etheric, and Soul Planes.

Satsang   A class in which students of ECK discuss a monthly lesson from Eckankar.

Self-Realization   Soul recognition. The entering of Soul into the Soul Plane and there beholding Itself as pure Spirit. A state of seeing, knowing, and being.

Shariyat-Ki-Sugmad   The sacred scriptures of Eckankar. The scriptures are comprised of twelve volumes in the spiritual worlds. The first two were transcribed from the inner planes by Paul Twitchell, modern-day founder of Eckankar.

Soul   The True Self, an individual, eternal spark

of God. The inner, most sacred part of each person. Soul can see, know, and perceive all things. It is the creative center of Its own world.

Soul Travel   The expansion of consciousness. The ability of Soul to transcend the physical body and travel into the spiritual worlds of God. Soul Travel is taught only by the Living ECK Master. It helps people unfold spiritually and can provide proof of the existence of God and life after death.

Sound and Light of ECK   The Holy Spirit. The two aspects through which God appears in the lower worlds. People can experience them by looking and listening within themselves and through Soul Travel.

Spiritual Exercises of ECK   Daily practices for direct, personal experience with the Sound Current. Creative techniques using contemplation and the singing of sacred words to bring the higher awareness of Soul into daily life.

Sri   A title of spiritual respect, similar to reverend or pastor, used for those who have attained the Kingdom of God. In Eckankar, it is reserved for the Mahanta, the Living ECK Master.

Sugmad *SOOG-mahd*   A sacred name for God. It is the source of all life, neither male nor female, the Ocean of Love and Mercy.

Twitchell, Paul An American ECK MASTER who brought the modern teachings of ECKANKAR to the world through his writings and lectures. His spiritual name is Peddar Zaskq.

Wah Z *WAH zee* The spiritual name of SRI HAROLD KLEMP. It means the secret doctrine. It is his name in the spiritual worlds.

Z *ZEE* Spiritual name for SRI HAROLD KLEMP. *See also* WAH Z.

For more explanations of ECKANKAR terms, see *A Cosmic Sea of Words: The ECKANKAR Lexicon*, by Harold Klemp.

About the Author

Award-winning author, teacher, and spiritual guide Sri Harold Klemp helps seekers reach their full potential.

He is the Mahanta, the Living ECK Master and spiritual leader of Eckankar, the Path of Spiritual Freedom. He is the latest in a long line of spiritual Adepts who have served throughout history in every culture of the world.

Sri Harold teaches creative spiritual practices that enable anyone to achieve life mastery and gain inner peace and contentment. His messages are relevant to today's spiritual needs and resonate with every generation.

Sri Harold's body of work includes more than one hundred books, which have been translated into eighteen languages and won multiple awards. The miraculous, true-life stories he shares lift the veil between heaven and earth.

In his groundbreaking memoir, *Autobiography of a Modern Prophet*, he reveals secrets to spiritual success gleaned from his personal journey into the heart of God.

Find your own path to true happiness, wisdom, and love in Sri Harold Klemp's inspired writings.